...So You Want To Plan a Birthday Party

Catherine A. Durkin
Sally A. Willette
Ann D. Wyles

photographs
  Charles D. Winters

illustrations
  Roger T. Sobkowiak

Atheneum
  New York   1980

... SO YOU WANT TO PLAN A BIRTHDAY PARTY!

Library of Congress Cataloging in Publication Data

Durkin, Catherine A
    So you want to plan a birthday party.
    SUMMARY: Four basic party plans (with many
adaptations), each for a different age child, with all
the necessary information on invitations, guest lists,
games, food, and favors. Includes recipes.
    1. Children's parties—Juvenile literature.
2. Birthdays—Juvenile literature. 3. Cookery—
Juvenile literature. 4. Entertaining—Juvenile
literature. [1. Parties. 2. Birthdays]
I. Willette, Sally A., joint author. II. Wyles,
Ann D., joint author. III. Title.
GV1205.S58   793.2′1   79-22277

Published simultaneously in Canada by McClelland & Stewart, Ltd.
Manufactured by Halliday Lithograph Corporation
West Hanover and Plympton, Massachusetts
First Edition

DEDICATED TO ALL CHILDREN
WHO LIKE TO HAVE A GOOD TIME
TOGETHER

ACKNOWLEDGMENTS

Thank you to the children who came to the parties photographed for this book. Other children can learn how to plan a party and play party games better by seeing these pictures.

We also appreciate very much the excellent illustrations of Roger T. Sobkowiak, the valuable layout counsel of T. Gerald Brooks, and the delightful and skilled photographic work of Charles D. Winters.

PREFACE

If you want to plan a party at home, this book should be a big help!

There are ideas and directions for games, recipes, invitations, decorations, placecards, and themes. There are many party tips, including some on feelings, so that you, your friends, and family will feel good about your party.

It doesn't have to cost much to have a fun party. Most of the fun comes from playing and being together.

Have a nice party!

What's In This Book

PLANNING BEFORE THE PARTY

 = prepare before the party

 = game

 = food

1

INVITATIONS

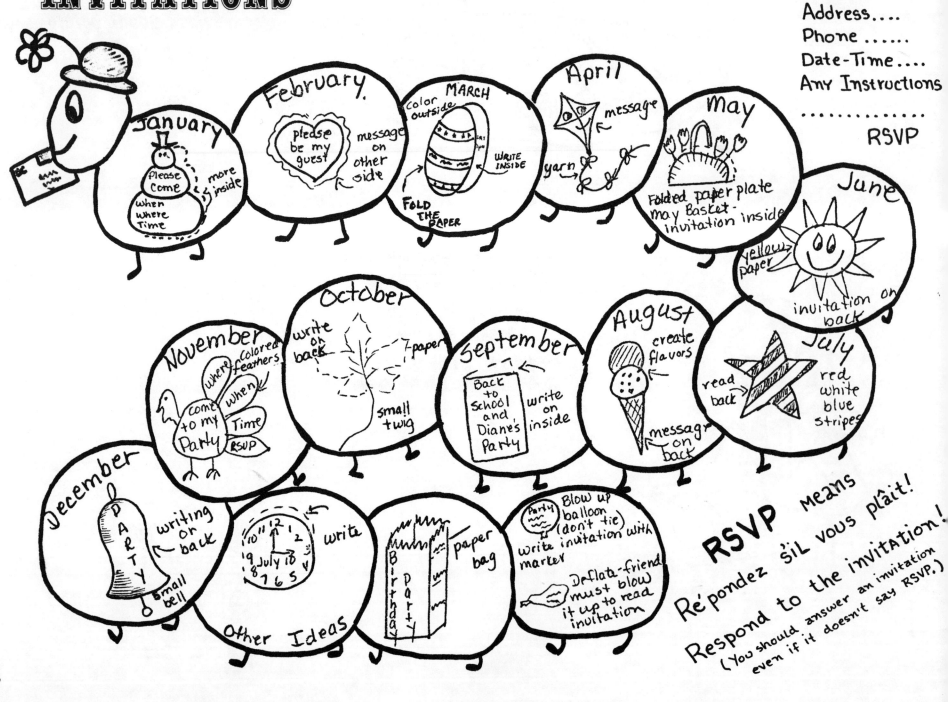

Name......
Address....
Phone ......
Date-Time....
Any Instructions
....
RSVP

January — Please Come, When Where Time — more inside

February. — please be my guest — message on other side

MARCH — Color outside — WRITE INSIDE — FOLD THE PAPER

April — message — yarn

May — Folded paper plate may Basket - invitation inside

June — yellow paper — invitation on back

July — read back — red white blue stripes

August — create flavors — message on back

September — Back to School and Diane's Party — write on inside

October — write on back — paper — small twig

November — where colored feathers — Come to my Party — when Time RSVP

December — PARTY — writing on back — small bell

Other Ideas — 10 11 12 1 2 July — write

Birthday Party — paper bag

Party Blow up balloon (don't tie) write invitation with marker. Deflate-friend must blow it up to read invitation

RSVP MEANS
Répondez s'il vous plâit!
Respond to the invitation!
(You should answer an invitation even if it doesn't say RSVP.)

2

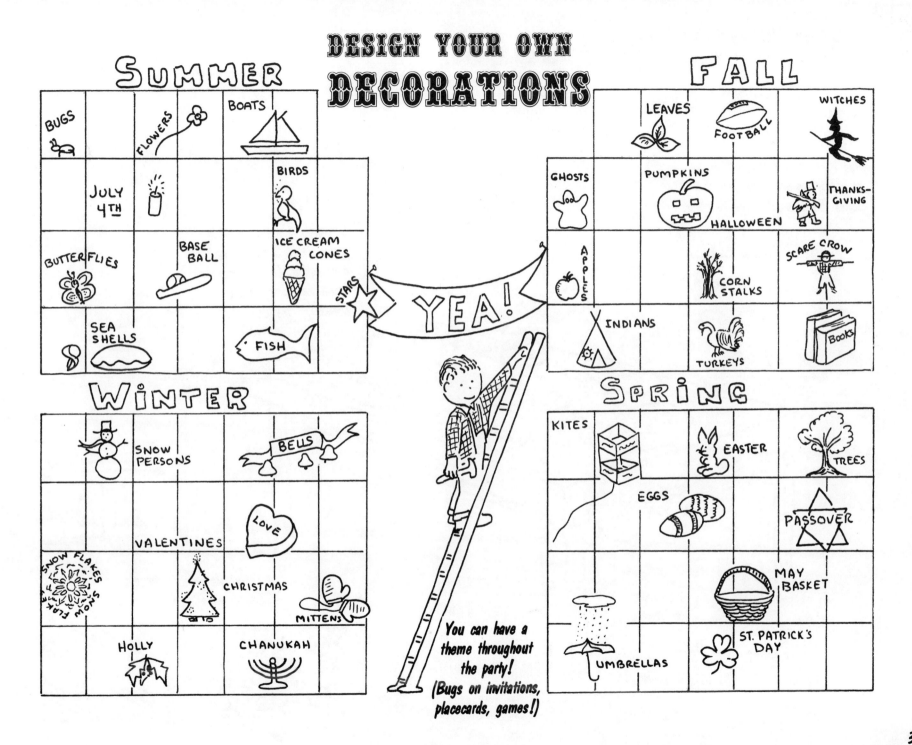

DESIGN YOUR OWN DECORATIONS

Summer

BUGS

FLOWERS

BOATS

JULY 4TH

BIRDS

BUTTERFLIES

BASE BALL

ICE CREAM CONES

SEA SHELLS

FISH

STARS

YEA!

Fall

LEAVES

FOOTBALL

WITCHES

GHOSTS

PUMPKINS

HALLOWEEN

THANKS-GIVING

APPLES

CORN STALKS

SCARE CROW

INDIANS

TURKEYS

Books

Winter

SNOW PERSONS

BELLS

LOVE

VALENTINES

SNOW FLAKES

CHRISTMAS

MITTENS

HOLLY

CHANUKAH

Spring

KITES

EASTER

TREES

EGGS

PASSOVER

MAY BASKET

UMBRELLAS

ST. PATRICK'S DAY

You can have a theme throughout the party! (Bugs on invitations, placecards, games!)

SET YOUR OWN TABLE

Use comic pages from newspaper or brown grocery bags. Trim the edges like this ⌄ ; tape together.

Use an old sheet or shelf paper. Draw a plate, cup, and napkin. Lay out crayons or markers and let your friends do the decorating.

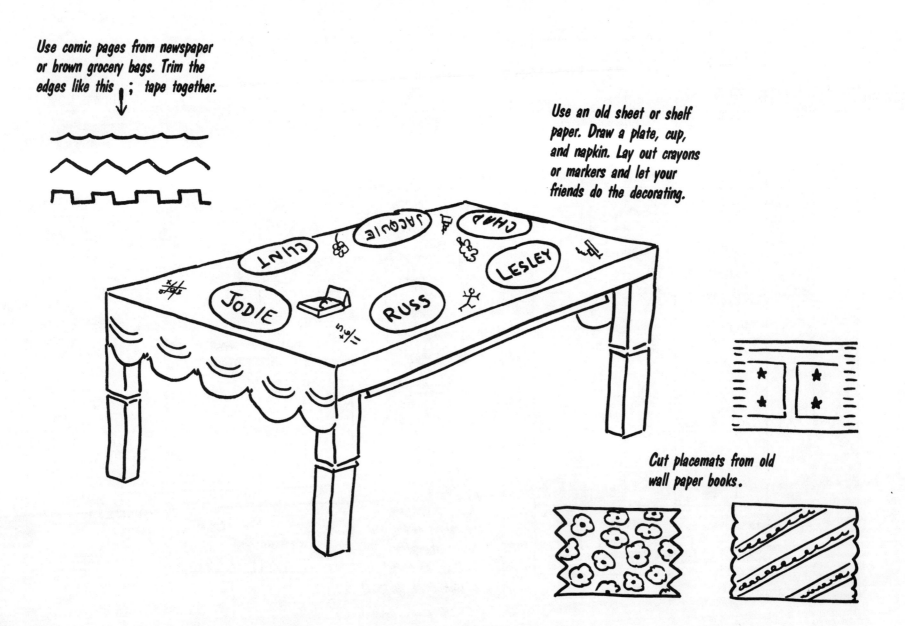

Cut placemats from old wall paper books.

ARRANGE YOUR OWN
CENTERPIECES

 Balloons taped to table

 Toys, dolls or stuffed animals

 Branches anchored in a pot with clay. Put guests' names on branches.

 Cake or other refreshments

 Wrapped favors

 Flowers, leaves or pine in water

5

PREPARE YOUR OWN PLACECARDS

Straw with Theme on It (Name on Back)

MARIA

Folded Paper with Your Own Design

Jean

J J

Name on Paper Plate, Cup and Napkin

PHILIP

Balloon Taped to Chair

They avoid confusion and hurt feelings. The kids enjoy the seating surprise, too!

JOHN

Indian Teepees

MAUREEN

Tooth Pick, Twig or Popsicle Stick Sign Stuck in Clay

PAT

Empty Spools with Paper Flowers

SNACKS

These could serve as main items or just as munchies at your party.

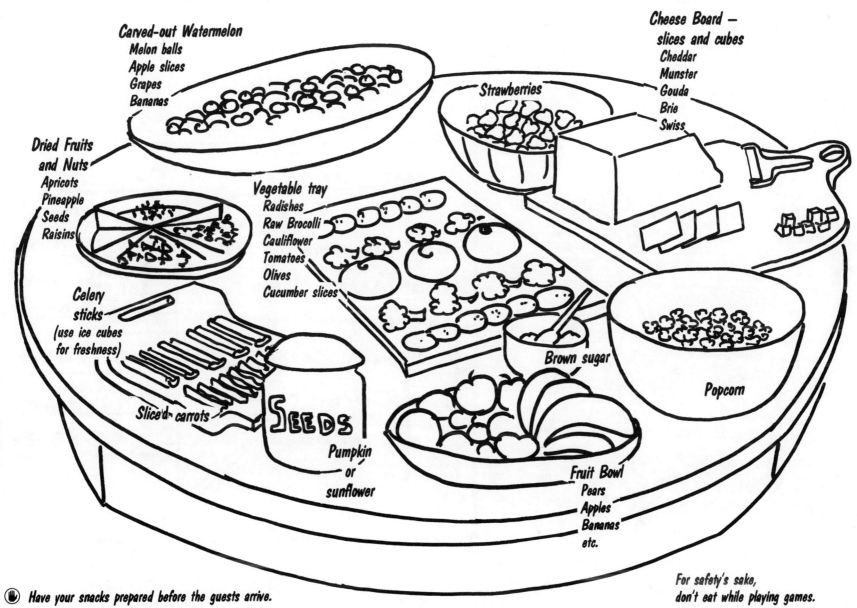

Carved-out Watermelon
Melon balls
Apple slices
Grapes
Bananas

Cheese Board —
slices and cubes
Cheddar
Munster
Gouda
Brie
Swiss

Strawberries

Dried Fruits and Nuts
Apricots
Pineapple
Seeds
Raisins

Vegetable tray
Radishes
Raw Brocolli
Cauliflower
Tomatoes
Olives
Cucumber slices

Celery sticks
(use ice cubes for freshness)

Slice'd carrots

Brown sugar

Popcorn

SEEDS
Pumpkin or sunflower

Fruit Bowl
Pears
Apples
Bananas
etc.

✋ Have your snacks prepared before the guests arrive.

For safety's sake, don't eat while playing games.

MAKE A LIST
OF WHAT YOU WANT
TO DO

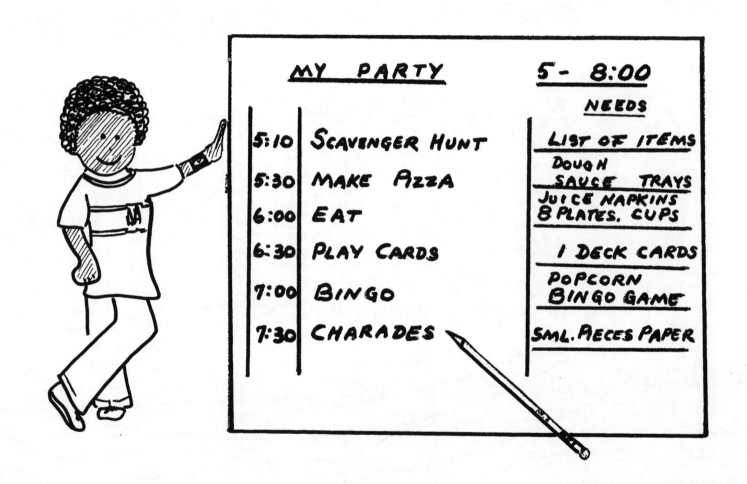

A
CLASSY
PARTY!

(the whole class
was invited!)

A PARTY FOR

5-6-7

YEAR OLDS

INVITATION

Cut a balloon shape out of construction paper, plain, or lined paper.

COME TO A PARTY!

AT: David John's 1931 Dove St Sat. Apr. 29 13:00

I filled in this part. It took a long time.

INSTEAD OF BUYING A GIFT, PLEASE BRING A USED, WRAPPED TOY, GAME OR BOOK TO TRADE.

The gift exchange was the favorite part of the party. We saved it till last.

I taped this string to the back of the invitation.

I invited the whole class!

10

MOLASSES CUPCAKES

MARGARET'S MARVELOUS MOLASSES CUPCAKES
(Makes 3 - 3-1/2 dozen — Bake 350° — 30 min.)

CREAM together:
1 cup sugar
1 cup shortening
3 eggs

ADD:
1 cup molasses
1 cup milk

ADD and stir WELL or BEAT:
3 cups flour
1 t. baking soda
1/2 t. baking powder
1 t. cinnamon
1 t. nutmeg
1 t. cloves
1 t. salt (scant)
1 t. vanilla

The day before the party we made 3 dozen (36) molasses cupcakes.
We did not ice them because we would do that at the party.

DECORATING THE OUTSIDE

I tied bright balloons out front so that everyone could find my house.

You could hang paper streamers or paper chains.

The party host or hostess could say "Hi! Glad you could come!" to each guest or something friendly like that.

The first guests arriving!

Every guest put the gift he or she brought into a numbered bag. (We had to borrow some bags!)

We used these bags at the end of the party for the gift exchange.

✋ Number your bags before the party, one for each guest. Put them all in the same area.

WHO'S GOT THE RING?

You have to look closely to see "who's got the ring."
A ring is passed around on a string. You try to pass
it to the next person without the detective spotting
it. Everyone should keep her/his hands moving on the
string to fool the detective! If the detective spots
you with the ring, you become the next detective.

Detective

The Ring

Tie the string together.

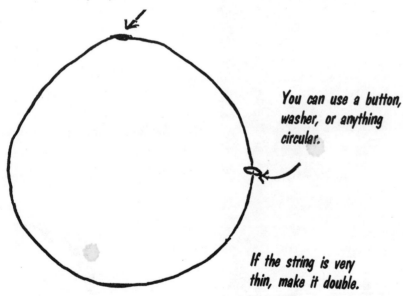

You can use a button,
washer, or anything
circular.

If the string is very
thin, make it double.

✋ Have a string (and ring) tied
and ready before the party.

This was a fun game.
We divided into 4 teams. Each team
had to find its own paper baby animals.
When you found your baby, you
brought it to your team captain.

The animals were cut out of
construction paper. It helped
the children to have a tiny one
to carry so they could match it
to what they found.

Cut out the animals and
ask someone to hide
them before the party.

This team had to
find baby horses.

THE MASKED TOUCH!

The person whose eyes were covered, reached out with a wand. When she touched someone, the person touched made a noise like an animal. The masked person guessed who it was. (If you didn't guess correctly, you tried again.)

The wand is a rolled newspaper page, taped at each end.

She said "wuff wuff"

Have your wand and scarf ready before the party.

16

You will need 2 brooms and 2 rocks. Divide everyone into 2 teams. The sweeper on each team must sweep the rock over a line. When you cross the line, your judge will say "okay." Then sweep the rock back to your line and the next person goes.

Don't make them sweep too far.

You can use a peanut, or whatever you wish.

You will need a chalk line or string taped down.

Have 2 chairs or stools for the judges.

Have your brooms, rocks, chalk, and chairs ready before the party. ✋

JUDGE A   JUDGE B

ICING CUPCAKES

He showed us how to
unwrap the cupcakes and ice them.

We iced our own cupcakes. We needed
extra knives. Some of us shared. We
took off the cupcake wrappers and
iced the cupcakes UPSIDE DOWN.

IVAN'S ICING (Vanilla)

1 stick (1/2 c.) butter or margarine (softened)
1 box confectioners sugar
1 t. salt
1 t. vanilla
Add milk till smooth enough to spread easily.

For chocolate, add 3 tablespoons cocoa to this recipe.
(The chocolate was delicious on the molasses cupcakes!)

Have your dishes of icing ready before the party.

We had 2 dishes of icing. (We should
have had 4) ... chocolate and vanilla.

I needed some help.

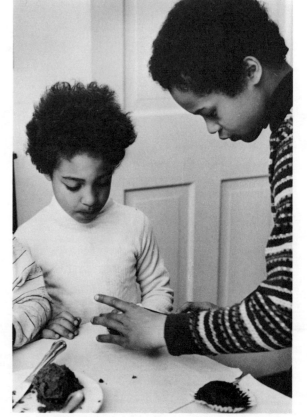

FROSTING THE JUICE GLASSES

Everyone liked fixing the glasses
before the juice was poured.

First: tip the glass upside down
in lemon juice.

Second: KEEP THE GLASS UPSIDE DOWN
and dip it into confectioners sugar.

Then add juice.

Lemon Juice   Confectioners Sugar

For drinks we had:

LENNY'S LEM-ORANGE
(20-25 6 oz. servings)

MIX: 1 large (12 oz.) can frozen lemonade
      1 large can frozen orange juice

Add water according to directions on can.
You can add sliced oranges or lemons.

For a small group, just mix 1 small can lemonade
with 1 small can orange juice.

✋ Before the party have 1 dish of lemon juice ready
and 1 dish confectioners sugar. Also have enough
glasses ready. They don't have to match.

TIME TO EAT

The balloons were taped near the ceiling and hung down.

We put a card table beside a long table.

As a snack before everyone ate, there were brown and golden RAISINS in PAPER CUP HOLDERS at everyone's plate.

We used the kitchen dishes and nothing got broken!

Before the party we put place markers at everyone's seat.

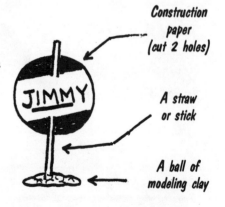

Construction paper (cut 2 holes)

A straw or stick

A ball of modeling clay

✋ Before the party, have enough placemarkers, dishes, chairs and table space ready.

PARTY HAT

The party hats were easy to make. My older brother made most of them. We used newspapers (mostly the Sunday funnies because they were colorful).

We TAPED THEM at the top so they wouldn't fall apart.

PETER AND PAM'S PARTY HAT

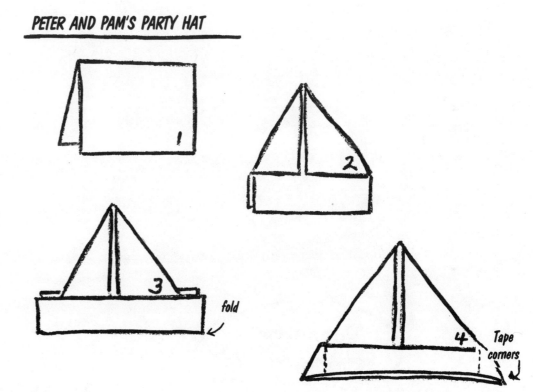

fold

Tape corners

✋ Make all your party hats before the party ... unless you are going to show the children how to do it. (Small children might find it difficult.)

SURPRISE GUEST

My Dad dressed up as a clown
and surprised us.

He found a penny on everyone!
Sometimes the penny was in a
person's hair!
(He wore gloves and kept the pennies
in his fist and worked them up to
his fingers one at a time.)

Jennifer

A surprise guest could bring a bag of gifts
(like painted rocks 😊) for everyone.

OTHER SURPRISE GUESTS

Dog carrying
basket of favors

This is a fun chance for a relative,
friend, or neighbor to "dress-up!"

Fun dances:
Mexican hat dance
Hokey pokey
Bunny hop

Gym teacher to
lead games

ATHLETIC
DEPT

36

Dance teacher to show
some old or new steps.
(You can get dance records
from the library.)

A pirate with favors
in homemade treasure
chest.

Small disc jockey
to play records
for games or dance.

ear-muffs

Remember: don't tell anyone
that a SURPRISE guest is coming!
Know in advance what time your
surprise will arrive.

23

BUTTON-BUTTON, WHO'S GOT THE BUTTON?

?   ?   ?

Everyone sat in a circle. One person walked around and pretended to slip a button into each person's hands (everyone folded her/his hands together). The button, though, was DROPPED into only 1 person's hands.*

When the person with the button sat down, everyone guessed who had the button.

The person with the button was "it" the next time.

*If you are "it" don't stop right after you drop the button. Pass a few more people and pretend to drop it.

✋ Have 1 button ready.

PUPPET SHOW

My brother and his friend gave a funny puppet show.
They just used stuffed animals and dolls we had at home.
They used a nursery rhyme and added an extra character.

It helps if the children can be seated on the floor and the puppets up high enough to be seen easily.

✋ *The "Puppet Show" entertainers should practice before the party and know the story they want to tell. The audience enjoys it when the puppets ask them questions.*

A PUPPET SHOW

This is a story that you could use for your puppet show. You can say it in your own words and decide on your own puppets or dolls.

If your guests can use sock puppets to be Rocko's cousins, they might enjoy that.

You can make the show long or short.

For scenery, use props from home or draw on paper.

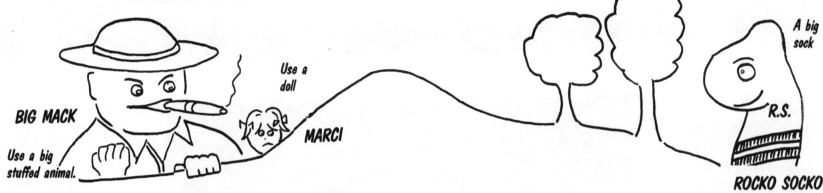

BIG MACK

Use a big stuffed animal.

Use a doll

MARCI

A big sock

R.S.

ROCKO SOCKO

GOLDEN GRASS HILL

Sweet Rocko Socko and his cousins live peacefully on Golden Grass Hill, (G.G. Hill).

Big Mack wants to cut down all the trees and put big buildings on G.G. Hill.

Everyone is sad on G.G. Hill. They need some good ideas to save their homes. Paco suggested making part of the mountain into a place for the city people. Rocko needs ideas from all of the cousins.

Every time Big Mack comes to G.G. Hill, he brings his little girl, Marci. She is very shy and lonely. One day when Marci came, Docko (who was also shy) waved to her. She waved back. Rocko Socko came over to them and talked about their sadness about losing the mountain.

Rocko asked his cousins for their ideas on making a park on the hill. (Audience participation.) Marci listened and looked surprised.

Every time Big Mack came back, Marci ran to watch the Sockos as they planted flowers, built benches, dug a pond, and made picnic tables and swings. Sometimes the cousins pushed Marci in a wheelbarrow!

One day Big Mack followed Marci and was shocked! He saw her laughing and running. He had never seen her so happy.

Big Mack knew then that he had made a big mistake. He decided to fix up old buildings downtown instead.

The Sockos and Marci sang "For He's a Jolly Good Fellow." Big Mack sang, too, and laughed.

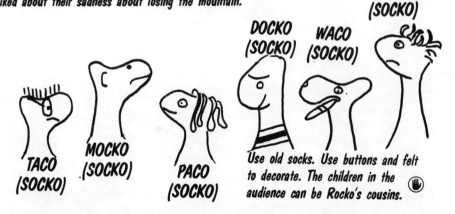

TACO (SOCKO)

MOCKO (SOCKO)

PACO (SOCKO)

DOCKO (SOCKO)

WACO (SOCKO)

JOCKO (SOCKO)

Use old socks. Use buttons and felt to decorate. The children in the audience can be Rocko's cousins.

THE GIFT EXCHANGE!
WE DIDN'T NEED FAVORS
AT THIS PARTY

Everyone got a number. When the puppet
called your number, you had to bring
your number to the puppet. (The puppet
took the numbers in his mouth!)
Then the puppet gave you the bag (with
a gift in it). Lots of people liked
their gifts and some traded.

Have enough numbers to pass out to the children. ✋
Have an extra wrapped gift or 2 ready in case of confusion.

27

A GROUP PHOTO

This was a fun day!
It was nice to be
together at my house!

We watched as one of my friends
made a balloon dance!

It's nice to snap a picture of the group.
It's fun to look at later.

A LUNCH AND MUNCH PARTY

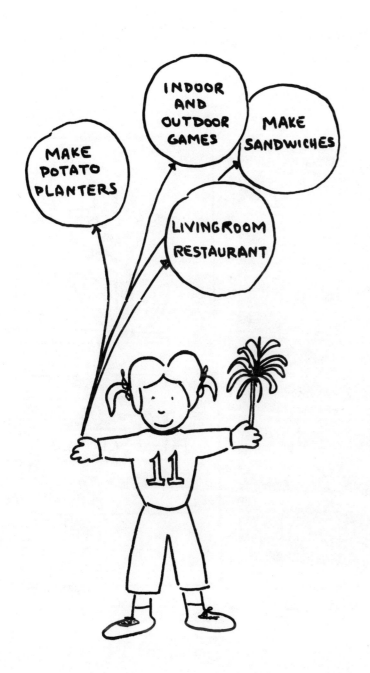

MAKE POTATO PLANTERS

INDOOR AND OUTDOOR GAMES

MAKE SANDWICHES

LIVINGROOM RESTAURANT

A PARTY FOR

7-8-9

YEAR OLDS

SPRING INVITATION

COME TO JOCELYN'S PARTY

MAY 10
12:00 - 2:00
131 N. 6th; 1st floor,
Luncheon
RSVP

In two weeks I will have my 9th birthday.
I'll send my invitations a week before the party.

I went to a wallpaper store near my apartment. The owner showed me some old wallpaper books that we could use to make placemats.

Have pages torn out and scissors ready before the guests arrive. ✋

HELPING SISTER

On the morning of the party, my sister and I hung our door decoration.

It looked just like my invitation, only bigger!

My sister was my helper for the party.
(Sometimes brothers and sisters feel bad when it isn't their party.)

Until all the guests arrived we kept busy trying to guess how many pennies were in the jar. Each girl wrote her guess on a piece of paper.

(You could also guess the number of beans, buttons, or anything else!)

Have jar of pennies, pencils, and pieces of paper ready beforehand. ✋

33

PIN THE BEE ON THE STAMEN

Each guest was blindfolded and turned 3 times. Then she tried to tape a paper bee on the stamen (the part of the flower the bee likes to sit on).

We used the door decoration for this game.

You can tape cotton balls on a bunny, feathers on a turkey, or tails on animals. Use your imagination.

One guest didn't like to be blindfolded so she helped to spin the other players. Don't force anyone to play.

MEMORY GAME

One party friend passed a tray around with 20 items taped to it. We all looked for 2 minutes ...

Then she took the tray away and we tried to write down what we remembered.

WRITING WHAT WE REMEMBERED

If we couldn't spell it, we drew it.

It wasn't easy!

Have the tray prepared ahead of time. ✋
The "passer" can select some items for the tray.

ANOTHER PAPER GAME:

Each person gets a piece of
paper. Fold paper into 4 parts.

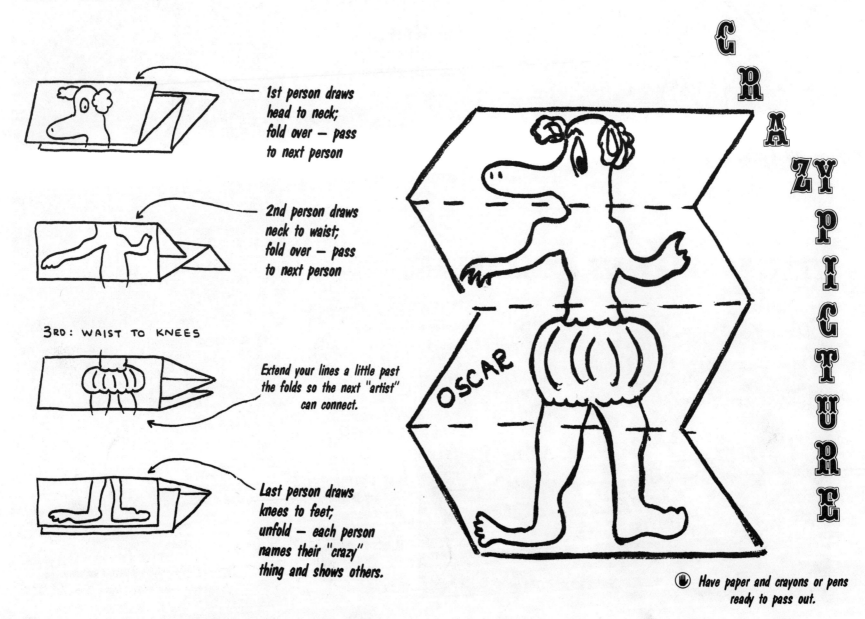

1st person draws
head to neck;
fold over — pass
to next person

2nd person draws
neck to waist;
fold over — pass
to next person

3RD: WAIST TO KNEES

Extend your lines a little past
the folds so the next "artist"
can connect.

Last person draws
knees to feet;
unfold — each person
names their "crazy"
thing and shows others.

GRAZY PICTURE

OSCAR

✋ Have paper and crayons or pens
ready to pass out.

36

I received many nice gifts.
I thanked each person after I opened
her gift.

My friends seemed just as excited
as I was. They liked watching me
open the gifts they brought.

GIFT IDEAS

There are many clever things to make or buy.

NAILS

Small bag with sample size shampoo, lotion, etc.

NOTIONS

GAME

Watch for sales!

Compass

N E

Pitcher and juice glasses

Collection starters, like a brass bell, box for post cards, coin or stamp books.

POST CARDS

WHIZ KID

Clothes

SCRAP BOOK

Record

TOOTH PASTE

Soaps, bath toys wrapped in washcloth.

Books

BIRTHDAY PARTY BOOK

Instrument or piano books

Stuffed animal

AUTO GRAPHS

Slate

Jewelry

MUSIC

PLACE MATS

To make our pretend-restaurant look pretty for lunch, we each chose a sample page from a discontinued wallpaper book to use as a placemat. We cut and trimmed the edges.

✋ Have wallpaper pages and scissors ready.

FIXING SANDWICHES

Using metal cookie cutters, or empty cans, or jars we cut out bread shapes. Then we spread them with egg salad, ham, tuna, or peanut butter and jelly.

I made 3 for myself!

We saved the scraps for bread crumbs and stuffing. The birds got some, too.

EDDIE'S EGG SALAD

6 hard boiled eggs
3 T. mayonnaise
1 t. mustard
1 t. seasoned salt
1 oz. cream cheese

Mash eggs with a fork or potato masher until egg pieces are small. Add other ingredients. Keep refrigerated. (1 egg/person)

How to hard boil eggs: put eggs in a pot of cold water. Bring to a rolling boil. Turn off heat. Cover. Leave eggs in pot for 15 minutes. Put in cold water. Eggs are easier to shell if done immediately.

Have bread, spreads, knives, and cutters ready.

VALERIE'S VANILLA SHAKES

(3 or 4 small shakes)
1 qt. (32 oz.) milk
3 scoops vanilla ice cream
Whirl quickly in blender.
. . . the more ice cream the better!

You can add chocolate or berries or different kinds of ice cream.

41

LIVING ROOM/RESTAURANT

Our miniature restaurant was set up in our living room.
We borrowed some chairs and tables and cut field flowers
for centerpieces.

While we were
in the dining room
making sandwiches,
Dad set up the tables.

BENJI'S BLUEBERRY PIE (serves 8)
Wash and drain 4 cups of blueberries.
1/4 cup water
5 T. flour
pinch salt
1 cup sugar
1/2 cup water

Make a smooth paste from 1/4 cup water and 5 T. flour, salt. Boil 1 cup berries 1 cup sugar, 1/2 cup water. Add paste and stir until thick. Add remaining 3 cups of berries. Cool. Pour in graham cracker crust. (Top with whipped cream.)

GODFREY'S GRAHAM CRACKER CRUST
Makes 1 - 9 inch crust:

Roll or crush 1 package of graham crackers (about 12 crackers) into fine crumbs. (Putting the crackers in a plastic bag makes rolling less messy.)

Add: 1/4 cup sugar
        1/4 cup melted margarine or butter

Mix well with a fork. Pour into 9" pie plate. Press firmly by putting an 8" pie plate inside. Remote 8" plate and bake for 8 minutes at 375°

I decided not to have a birthday cake. My favorite is blueberry pie.

My mother served it to us while my friends sang to me.

HAPPY BIRTHDAY TO YOU

SALADS AND CARROT CAKE

FRIEDA'S FRENCH DRESSING

1/4 cup sugar
1/2 t. dry mustard
1/2 t. garlic salt
1 cup tomato soup (undiluted)
1/2 cup vinegar
1 cup oil
MIX WELL (makes 3 cups)

For Dessert:
CASEY'S CARROT CAKE
(tastes like a spice cake)

Blend: 2 cups sugar
1-1/2 cups oil
Add: 3 eggs
Sift together and add to above:
2 cups flour
2 t. baking soda
1 t. salt
3 t. cinnamon
Add: 2 t. vanilla
2 cups raw carrots (grated)
Pour: into greased 2 layer pans, or 13x9x2 pan.
Bake: 350° 1 hour

CARLETON'S CREAM CHEESE FROSTING

Mix and frost cooled cake.
Beat 1 stick margarine, melted
or 1 8 oz. pkg. cream cheese
stir 1 lb. confectioners sugar
2 t. vanilla

IRVING'S ITALIAN DRESSING

2/3 cup oil
1/4 cup vinegar
2 T. water
1/4 t. salt
1/8 t. pepper
1/8 t. paprika
1/8 t. garlic powder
1/2 t. parsley
MIX AND SHAKE WELL (makes 1 cup)

44

SOME MORE DRINKS

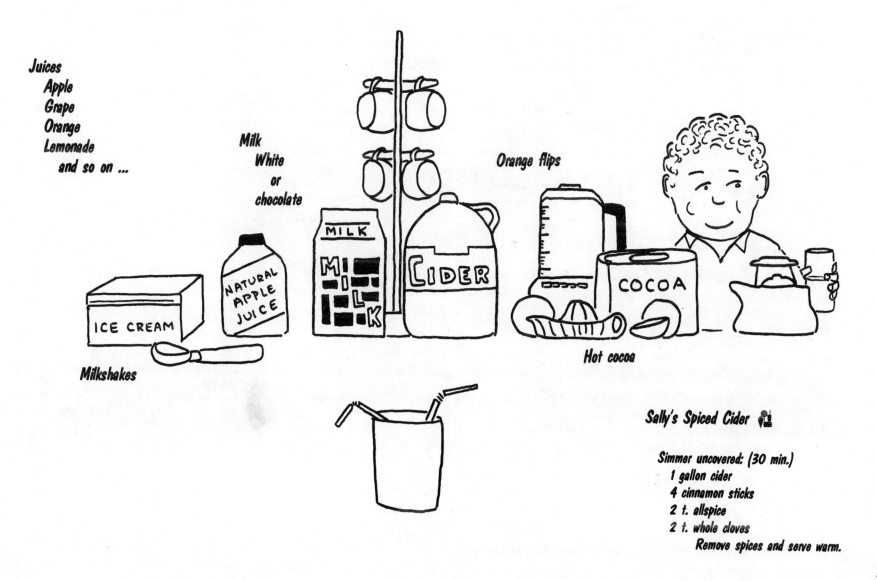

Juices
  Apple
  Grape
  Orange
  Lemonade
  and so on ...

Milk
  White
  or
  chocolate

Orange flips

Milkshakes

Hot cocoa

Sally's Spiced Cider

Simmer uncovered: (30 min.)
  1 gallon cider
  4 cinnamon sticks
  2 t. allspice
  2 t. whole cloves
  Remove spices and serve warm.

45

PLANTER FAVORS

My father showed us how to make our potato planters.

POTATO PLANTERS

Directions for one planter:
Needed: 1 potato (cut and scooped out by an older person)
3 thumbtacks for eyes and nose
4 golf tees for legs
1 pipe cleaner for curly tail
dirt
grass seed
name tag (to keep with the planter)

toothpick

✋ Potato should be scooped before the party and other supplies gathered.

In less than two weeks we'll be able to cut our planter's hair, I mean grass!!

CREATE YOUR OWN FAVORS

Fun to make at the party!

Small seashells or pretty stones on a mirror

Terrarium

Old jar

SEEDS

Friendship scarf

Plain material; each person signs name with crayon, iron between newspaper to fix.

MEGAN JAMIE KISHAN RAJI JOAN ANGELA HELGA BONNIE

SOAP JULIO

dried flower or weeds

Ring pictures — wooden curtain ring — Burlap glued to back

PENCILS & THINGS

Cover old can; decorate

Peanut people

Poke holes with needles — push pipe cleaner through (Thimbles would help)

buttons

Bean bag
Two pieces of felt or fabric filled with beans.

Bird feeder
Fill with seeds or crumbs

empty grapefruit

chestnuts: drill holes before party (vice needed)

NOTES

beans dyed in food coloring

Necklaces

Totem pole
cardboard roll

Party photo (given later) in frame

48

FAVOR USING BOTTLES

FABRIC FLOWERS
(This makes 9 flowers)

Need:
  1 yard fabric ribbon or spray-starched
  fabric — 3 inches wide
  9 pipe cleaners
  9 pom poms
  White glue

Instructions:
  Cut out fabric ribbon to match the pattern shown here. Fold ribbon like a fan (in many folds). Wrap pipe cleaner around the center of the fan. Secure tightly.
  Glue one pom-pom to center of the flower.
  Each child could make several. They look nice in the bottles!

FABRIC FLOWER PATTERN

Yarn

Rick-Rack

Find some old bottles. Soak (warm water is easiest) labels off.
Cut some sprigs of whatever's in season.
You could decorate them or your guests could! A nice "favor."
These bottles can double as table decorations and placemarkers.

OLD WITCH

You will love this game and play it for hours if you can just understand these directions!

OLD WITCH

The object of the game is for the Old Witch to correctly guess your category. When it's guessed, the player must run to catch the Witch. The first player to catch the Witch becomes the new Witch.

Instructions:

    1 person is the Old Witch

    1 person is the Door

    The rest are players

The players sit in a line on steps, a wall, grass, the driveway — anywhere. The Old Witch names a category that he/she wants (like "pies"). The witch then stands far away from the players.

The Door, now, goes to all the players to see what kind of pie they want to be. If you want to be "Raspberry Pie," whisper that to the Door. The Door makes certain that no 2 players have the same pie. Even the Door can pick a pie.

When everyone is ready, the Door goes out into the yard and faces the players. The Old Witch comes and knocks on the Door's back.

"Knock, Knock," says the Witch. "Do you have any pies?"

"Yes," says the Door. "Come and see." (The Door then sits down with the players.)

Then the Old Witch comes close to the players and starts to guess pie names. If she guesses "Raspberry," then that player must chase the Witch, around a goal and back to the line.

If you don't catch the Witch, the Witch guesses again (the Raspberry Pie tells the Door his/her new name and plays, too). The Witch can also name a new category. Start again.

THE OUTGOING WITCH BECOMES THE DOOR.

⚽ CAT AND MOUSE

We made a large circle. One girl was the cat
and another the mouse. The other girls held hands.
They let the mouse run in and out of the circle.
When the cat tried to get in or out, they tried
to stop her. When the cat caught the mouse, the
mouse became the cat and a new mouse was selected
by the outgoing cat.

JUMPING ROPE

Before all the girls went home,
we jumped rope.

They said: *Teddy Bear, Teddy Bear, turn around,*
Teddy Bear, Teddy Bear, touch the ground.

Teddy Bear, Teddy Bear, read the news,
Teddy Bear, Teddy Bear, tie your shoes.

Teddy Bear, Teddy Bear, go upstairs,
Teddy Bear, Teddy Bear, comb your hairs.
(or say your prayers)

Teddy Bear, Teddy Bear, turn out the lights,
Teddy Bear, Teddy Bear, say G-O-O-D N-I-G-H-T.

1 - 2 - 3 - 4 - 5
AND SO ON. . . .

These are my friends who
helped make my day special.

GOOD-BYE

Too soon I had to say
good-bye to my last guest.

SMALL PARTY

MAKE NECKLACE

MAKE SUNDAES

WATCH MOVIE

INDOOR GAMES

A PARTY FOR

9-10-11

YEAR OLDS

INVITATION

I delivered this invitation
to 7 of my friends.

COME
TO

MY
PARTY

Name __Holly__

Address __60 Elm St.__

Date __January 11__

Time __6:30 - 9:00__

RSVP
221-6868

BORROWING THE MOVIE FILM

My name is Holly. I will be 11 years old. Since I have a winter birthday, I decided to have a movie party. We got a film and projector from our local library to show at my house.

INTRODUCTIONS

I introduced everyone
when they arrived.

A GIFT

One friend brought me a plant.
It will look nice by the window
in my room.

I was really excited at my party but I tried to remember to say "thank you"
and tell them how I would use each gift. My friends seemed glad about that.

IMAGINATIVE GIFT WRAPPINGS

A CLEAR PLASTIC BAG AND YARN

WALL PAPER

WHITE PAPER WHICH YOU DECORATE

FOIL

BLACK AND WHITE NEWSPRINT

SUNDAY FUNNIES

PAPER BAGS AND STRING

HAPPY BIRTHDAY
TO REGGIE MARSH
CHICAGO, ILL

HOMEMADE BIRTHDAY CARDS

Plain paper
with drawing

Cartoon
mounted on paper
or
magazine cutouts
with your own caption

Recycled invitation
Use part of the invitation
and write on an empty side

Small piece of
wrapping paper
Write inside

Thumbprints or
fingerprints

GAME
TIME

⚽ ORANGE RELAY

The idea of this game is to pass the orange from one person to the next (under the chin and no hands allowed!)

We divided into 2 teams and formed 2 circles. We passed the orange around twice since we had such small circles.

The first team done is the winner. If the orange drops, pass it back one person and start again.

Have 2 oranges (or any other round fruit or ball) ready.

ELASTIC RELAY ⚽

This is a quick relay.
We had 2 teams. The girls
had to pass an elastic from
head to toe and back again,
then pass the elastic to
the next girl.

Since this game goes fast,
you might want to try it
twice (the second time,
start from the bottom up).

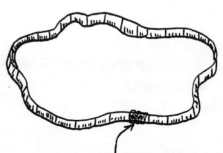

✋ Have ready 2 feet of elastic sewn together. One for each team.

PRIZES

Instead of prizes we played all of the games for peanuts. The first team got 10, the second team got 5.

Have ready a bowl of peanuts and bags for everyone.

WATCHING THE FUN

*It was as much
fun to watch as it
was to play.*

In this relay we had to put on crazy (my Dad's) clothes. Any funny clothes will do.

Included in each suitcase was a pair of pants, a hat, a shirt, and a pair of shoes. On 'Go' the 1st player ran to her suitcase, put clothes on, clapped 3 times,* took clothes off, ran to next player in line, and so on until a team won.

*You could ring a bell, horn or something else instead of clapping.

THE MOVIE

TREASURE AT THE MILL

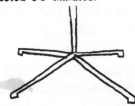

We all enjoyed the movie, popcorn, and cider. The film lasted 50 minutes.

WORD RBSALGME ☐ WORD SCRAMBLE

SCRAMBLE

1. BRGREUMAH
2. GDO THO
3. ENHCCIK
4. ZAZPI
5. GTTIEAPSH
6. CEI EMARC
7. ISEKICP
8. KAHESILKM
9. NHCERF FEISR
10. OONNIS

We tried to figure out mixed-up food words.

Have your word list, pencils and paper ready. ✋

FORTUNE ⚽

The girls loved writing fortunes.

Need:
Lots of small pieces
of paper, 10 small
bags, pencils.

Instructions:
There is a prepared fortune with certain words missing. Each player supplies the missing words which will be mixed up in a bag according to category. The reader will choose a word from the bag to fill in each blank.

Example:
"Write a boy's name." The player writes a boys name on her/his small piece of paper and puts it in the bag marked BOY'S NAME. Continue until all papers are in the bags.

YOUR NAME

BOY'S NAME

COLOR · COLOR · NUMBER · JOB · JOB · CITY · FOOD

GAME

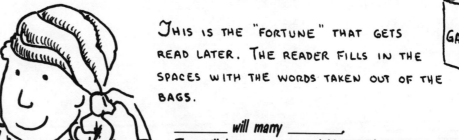

This is the "fortune" that gets read later. The reader fills in the spaces with the words taken out of the bags.

_____ will marry _____,
They will have _____ children with _____ eyes
and _____ hair.
_____ will be a _____ and _____ will be a _____,
They will live in _____, eat _____, and
play _____ all day long.

My Mom and Dad took turns reading
the funny fortunes! This was
Stacy's fortune:

Stacy will marry **Bobby**. They will have
48 children with **silver** eyes and **purple**
hair. *Stacy* will be a **doctor** and **Bobby** will
be a **ballerina**. They will live in **Miami**,
eat **pickles**, and play **monopoly** all day long.

It turned out to be very noisy fun!

69

SUNDAES

This is the yummy part of my party. We made our own sundaes.

BRIGID'S BUTTERSCOTCH SAUCE

1-1/2 cup brown sugar
1/2 cup light corn syrup
1/4 cup butter
1/2 cup cream
1 t. vanilla

Heat sugar, syrup, and butter over low heat to boiling. Stir constantly. Remove. Stir in cream and vanilla.

HOWIE'S HOT FUDGE SAUCE

2 squares melted, unsweetened chocolate
1 can condensed, sweetened milk
1/2 cup water

Stir together. Heat in double boiler. Thin with milk if it's too thick.

WANDA'S WHIPPED CREAM

1 8 oz. carton heavy cream
3 T. sugar (powdered is smoother than granulated)
1 t. vanilla

Beat cream till almost stiff, add sugar and vanilla.

We had small dishes of sauces, nuts, berries, and whipped cream.

*We all blew out
the candles on
my birthday cookies.*

SHANDRA'S SUGAR COOKIES

1 cup shortening
3 eggs
2 cups sugar
4 cups flour
1/4 cup milk
1 t. baking powder
1 t. baking soda
1 t. vanilla

Cream together shortening, eggs, and sugar. Add 2 cups flour and blend well.

Add milk, 2 cups flour, baking powder, baking soda, and vanilla. Mix well and roll out on floured surface.

Use cookie cutters to cut shapes or a glass rim for round cookies.

Bake at 350° for 8-10 minutes.

Make sure candles are secure.

NECKLACE FAVORS

Our favors were alphabet bead necklaces.

We bought the beads at a craft store. They were only a few cents each.

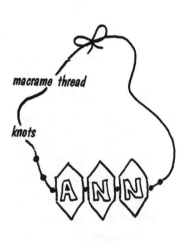

macrame thread

knots

A N N

✋ Put each girl's beads and thread in a bag or envelope before the party.

See how nice it looks!

SPILLS

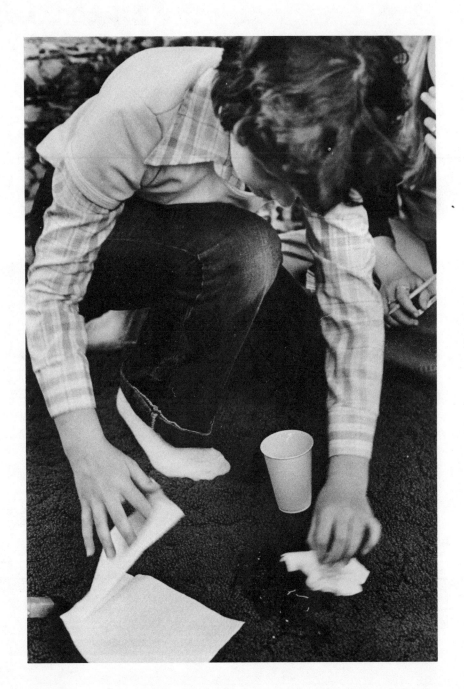

Accidents do happen!

Until the girls went home we tried
some of the latest dances.

If you are planning a
dance party, you could make
invitations like records.

TO DEBBIE
COME TO VICKY'S
●
FISKEHILL RD.
DEC. 18
5 - 7:00

Before the party I got my favorite records together.

A PICTURE FOR MY ALBUM

It was a GREAT party!

CHEFS AND CHARADES

Cooks
and
Cards?

SMALL PARTY

PLAY CARDS AND CHARADES

MAKE SUBMARINE SANDWICHES

SCAVENGER HUNT

A PARTY FOR

11-12

YEAR OLDS

INVITING BY PHONE

"Hello, Andy? This is Mike. Can you come to my party this Friday? It's from 5 to 8 o'clock and it's for dinner. Good! See you then. Bye."

There were more kids I would like to have invited, but this year my mom said I should have a small party.

I tried to get organized so that when my friends came, we'd have something to eat and something to do.

*At certain meat counters they make their own lunch meats without preservatives and artificial additives.

This was my grocery list:

9 submarine rolls
1 pound bologna
1/2 pound ham
1/2 pound salami*
1/2 pound sliced cheese
1 head lettuce
1 package tomatoes (3 or 4)

2 cans frozen grape juice

1 pound carrots
1 package celery
5 bananas
5 apples
5 oranges
1 box ice cream cones
1 qt. frozen yogurt

SCAVENGER HUNT ⚽

THE LIST

- WILLOW BRANCH
- PINE CONE
- PIECE OF MARBLE
- WORM
- BUG
- PIECE OF MOSS
- BIRCH BARK
- PIECE OF SLATE

✋ Have the lists ready
   ahead of time.

Checking the list!

This was the birch bark

and the pine cone

and slate.

The one who makes up the lists gets to be the "checker."
Everyone brought his items to him.

✋ Have bags handy for items found.

BINGO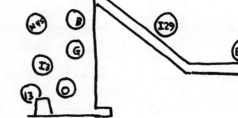

We took turns
being caller.

We used beans
for markers.

✋ Have bingo game on hand.

I DOUBT IT!

"I Doubt It" — a card game
Object — to get rid of all of your cards
Card rank — A (high), K Q J 10, etc.
Deal all the cards

The players must announce as they lay down cards (face down) that they are putting down as many Aces (or whatever) as cards. The players need not tell the truth. (The 1st player lays down Aces, the next Kings and so on. Then repeat.)

If another player doubts what you put down and you were correct, the doubter must pick up all the cards on the table. If you were not telling the truth, you pick up the cards.

*You could also play this game with Ace, low.
   Then, go to 2's, 3's, and so on.

Have deck of cards ready.
You could also play Hearts, Go Fish,
   Rummy, Crazy 8's, or other card games.

GRANDMOTHER

My grandmother enjoyed my friends and was a big help. She stayed for half of the party.

Everyone pitched in!

One boy cut the rolls,

one diced tomatoes,

one chopped 1/2 head lettuce,

one set the meat and cheese
    on a platter,

one poured drinks and got
    ice ready,

one got out mayonnaise, mustard,
    pickles, and vegetable oil.

Then everyone made his own sandwich.

We cleared the table and sat down
to eat together.

The kids made the sandwiches
the way they liked them.

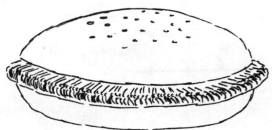

HEDDA'S HAMBURGERS

Mix together:
  1 lb. ground beef
  1 t. salt
  1/2 t. pepper
  1 T. parsley
  2 T. milk
  twist of lemon juice

Make patties, 6 thick ones or 8-9 thin ones.
Fry in heated pan or grill.
Serves 6

TIM'S TACOS

1 lb. ground beef, browned,
  and drained well.
Refried beans, optional
1 cup cheddar cheese, grated
1/2 head lettuce, chopped
4 tomatoes, cubed
Taco shells (can be bought)
Taco sauce

Put meat, beans, cheese, lettuce
and tomatoes in separate dishes
and let guests serve themselves.
(Serves 8)

SHELLS

TOMATOES   CHEESE   LETTUCE   SAUCE   BEEF

PABLO'S PIZZA

DOUGH FOR PIZZA
(This makes 2 trays and
serves 12; you can use
cookie sheets)

3-3 1/2 cups flour
1 T. sugar
1 t. salt
1/4 cup shortening
1 pkg. yeast
1 cup very warm water

Dissolve yeast in water.
Add shortening.
Add flour, sugar, and salt and mix.
Spread out on greased cookie trays.
Add sauce and cheese.
Bake at 425° till golden or 10-15 minutes.

PIZZA SAUCE

Simmer for 5 minutes:
1-6 oz. can tomato sauce
1-6 oz. can water
1 t. olive oil (or vegetable oil)
1/2 t. salt
1/2 t. pepper
1/2 t. oregano

Pour over pizza dough and
top with Mozzarella cheese

CHARADES

My sister wrote down some charades for us before the party. She wrote 12 for each team!

 TEAM X   TEAM Y

THE TEAMS CAN MAKE UP CHARADES FOR EACH OTHER. GO INTO SEPARATE ROOMS TO DO THIS.

3 minute time limit is best

You will need scraps of paper, 2 pencils, and a watch with a second hand.

Younger kids like to play 1-word charades (like "camera," "banana," etc.). It helps to have them ready ahead of time. Everyone can guess!!

88

Without talking:

1. Tell if it's a book, movie or song.

2. Tell how many words in the title.

3. Hold up your finger to tell which word you're acting out.

   (If you think you can act out the whole idea, then make a big circle in the air and then go from there.)

   When someone guesses your word, point to him/her and nod yes.

Other tips:

little word —

how many syllables —

Book:
   Open two hands

Movie:
   Make a ring with one hand over the eye — rotate other hand

Song:
   Move one hand away from the mouth

YOLANDA'S YOGURT CONES

We had raspberry yogurt.
Delicious!

SEE YOU LATER!

I thanked my friends, and my friends thanked me! I was glad we could be together.

FROSTING BIN

WENDY'S WHITE CAKE

2/3 cup butter
1-1/4 cups sugar
1 t. vanilla
1/2 t. almond extract (optional)
2-1/2 cups sifted cake flour
2-1/2 t. baking powder
2/3 cup milk
4 egg whites
1/2 t. salt
1/2 t. cream of tartar

Cream butter and sugar until fluffy. Add vanilla.

Sift together flour and baking powder.

Add to creamed mixture with milk.

Beat egg whites until foamy, add salt and cream of tartar. Fold into first mixture.

Pour into two 9" greased and floured pans.

Bake at 375° for 20-25 minutes.

CORA SUE'S COCOA CAKE

1 cup butter or margarine
2 cups sugar
4 eggs
3/4 cups cocoa
2 cups boiling water
3 cups flour
1 t. salt
2 t. baking powder
2 t. baking soda
2 t. vanilla

Cream together butter and sugar. Blend in eggs.

Add cocoa and boiling water alternately with flour, salt, baking powder, and soda.

Mix well. Add vanilla.

Bake in greased pan or pans at 350° for 20-30 minutes for layer cake, 45 minutes for 9"x13" pan.

You can refrigerate this cake.

DECORATIONS

Animal Crackers
Raisins
Nuts
Bananas — or other fruit
Chocolate chips
Coconut

YASMIN'S YELLOW CAKE

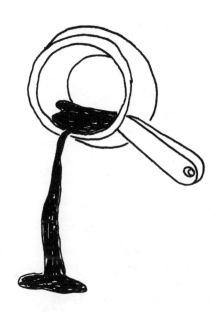

1/2 cup shortening, room temperature
1-1/2 cups sugar
2-1/2 cups flour
3/4 t. salt
1 cup milk
2 t. baking powder
3 eggs
1 t. vanilla
   Preheat oven at 350°

   Soften shortening with the mixer, add sugar, flour, and salt. Add 3/4 cup milk and beat 2 minutes. Add baking powder, eggs, remaining milk, and beat 1 minute. Add vanilla. Place in a greased and floured 9"x 13" pan and bake 30-40 minutes or divide into 2 or 3 9" cake pans that have been greased and floured and bake for 20 minutes.

FRED'S FLUFFY FROSTING

2 egg whites
3/4 cup brown sugar
1/3 cup light corn syrup
2 T. water
1/4 t. cream of tartar
1/4 t. salt

   Put all ingredients in top of double boiler.
   Beat with beater over boiling water until mixture stands in peaks and is thick enough to spread.

INEZ'S ICE CREAM CAKE

1/2 gallon of favorite ice cream
Enough lady fingers or cookies
   to cover ice cream
Favorite sauce

   Unwrap ice cream and cover with lady fingers or cookies.
   Freeze until ready to serve.
   Slice and serve with sauce.

FELIX'S FUDGE FROSTING

1-12 oz. package of semi-sweet
   chocolate pieces
3 T. butter
1/2 cup powdered sugar
1/2 cup evaporated milk
1 t. vanilla
1/4 t. salt

   Melt chocolate pieces with butter over low heat.
   Remove from heat. Add sugar, milk, vanilla and salt.
   Beat until smooth.
   See page 18 for another chocolate frosting.

CAROLYN'S COFFEE CAKE

1/2 cup margarine
1-8 oz. package cream cheese
1-1/4 cups sugar
2 eggs
1 t. vanilla
1/2 cup milk
2 cups flour
2 t. baking powder
1/2 t. baking soda
1/2 t. salt

Cream margarine and cheese, add sugar, eggs and vanilla.

Sift together flour, baking powder, soda, and salt.

Add to creamed mixture with milk.

Pour into greased 9x13 pan. Sprinkle with crumb topping.

CRUMB TOPPING

1/4 cup butter or margarine
1/2 cup flour
1/2 cup brown sugar
1/2 cup nuts

Mix together.
Bake at 350° for 30-40 min.

POLLY'S POUND CAKE

3 cups sugar
2 sticks butter
1/2 cup shortening
4 eggs
3 cups flour
1/2 t. baking powder
1 cup milk

Cream together sugar, butter, and shortening.

Add eggs, well beaten.

Sift together flour and baking powder. Add to creamed mixture, alternating with milk.

Pour into greased tube pan.

Bake at 350° for 1 hour.

SIDNEY'S SHORTCAKE

2 cups flour
3 t. baking powder
3/4 t. salt
5 T. granulated sugar
1 t. grated lemon or orange rind (optional)
1/2 cup shortening
1 egg, beaten
1/3 cup milk

Preheat oven to 450°

Sift together flour, baking powder, salt, and sugar. Add the rind.

With pastry blender or 2 knives, mix shortening with the flour mixture and add egg to make the dough easier to handle.

Roll or pat dough into 1/2" thick round to fit into a greased 9" layer pan. Bake 15-20 minutes.

You may cut individual pieces and put crushed berries on top. Or, you may slice the whole cake in half and put half the berries in the middle section, cover with other half of cake and top with remainder of berries and whipped cream.

Blueberries, strawberries, raspberries, or peaches may be used for the topping.

Use Your Imagination

*You Can Make Up
Your Own Party
Names and Themes*

Here are some extra parties.
After you decide on your
party theme, go through the
book and find the games,
menu, and other activities
that you would enjoy.

ANOTHER PARTY IDEA

NATURE RELAY ⚽

This is a relay game where the first players in each line run up to a bag and pick out a certain object. They show it to the "bag person," and then run back to tag the next person.

Need: 2 bags (or more depending on the number of teams)
Objects for bag (like an acorn, rock, pine cone, etc.) Each bag contains the same number of objects.
Lists of objects — to be held by "bag persons."
There are players in lines, and a "bag person" for each team (line).

Instructions: When a player runs up to the bag, the "bag person" (behind the bag) reads the first item on the list. The player reaches into the bag and pulls out the item. When the "bag person" says "OKAY," the player returns the item to the bag and runs back to his/her line to tag the next person. The game continues until everyone has a chance to find an object.

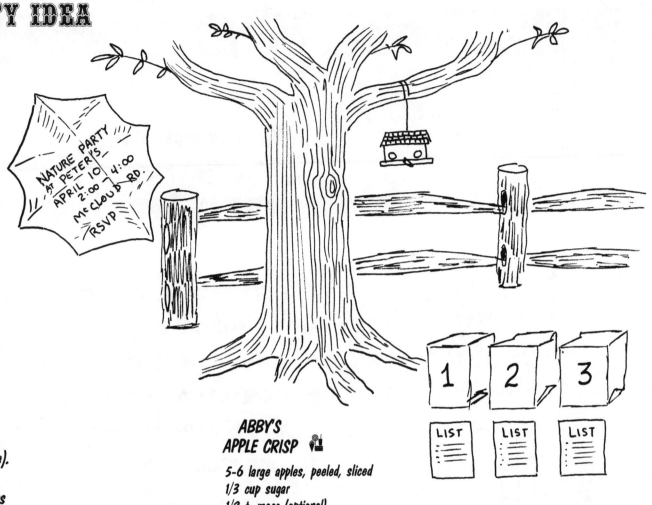

ABBY'S APPLE CRISP

5-6 large apples, peeled, sliced
1/3 cup sugar
1/2 t. mace (optional)
1 t. cinnamon
1/2 t. nutmeg
Mix all together.
Pour into 8x8 pan.

Blend and sprinkle on top:
1 cup brown sugar
1 cup flour
1/2 cup butter
Bake 350° — 45 minutes

CLARENCE'S CHEESE DIP FOR VEGETABLES

12 oz. cream cheese
1/4 cup mayonnaise
1/3 cup parmesan
1/4 t. oregano
1/8 t. garlic powder

The fresh air and nature games
will perk you up and put you in touch
with what's happening this season!

NATURE DAY

GAME — SNATCH IT

This game is played in 2 lines,
with 1 person from each side
attempting to get an object from
the center which the leader has
named. Players on both sides
have numbers.

Need: 4 objects from nature
example: rock, stick, acorn,
pine cone

Instructions: 2 teams, line up
across from each other with
objects in middle

Each team numbers off.
The leader calls — "No. 2 - rock"
The team whose "No. 2" snatches
    the rock 1st, gets a a point.
Leader calls numbers and keeps
    score.

ALPHABET HIKE

Each team gets a card with A to Z.
Teams go on walk and look for
an A item, B item, C item, etc.
Leader writes it down.

NATURE
A
B
C
D
E
F

Adapt other games
to the outdoor theme.

A WATER PARTY

COME TO A
WATER PARTY
AT CADDY'S
2204 ADMIRAL DR.
SUNDAY AUG. 29
12 – 2:00 (FOR LUNCH TOO)
BRING A BATHING SUIT AND TOWEL!

WATER GAMES: 🔘

Jump the water (someone holds the hose; the water spray keeps getting higher).
Dunk for apples
Water balloon toss

A wading pool is fun.

RELAY RACES: 🔘

Walk with a spoonful of water and put it in a glass at the other side.

Two teams sweep water-filled balloons. See whose lasts the longest (one balloon for each team.)

Fill the balloons before the party. Fill plenty because kids like to play it a few times.

Have a lunch and water party with outside games. This is a great way to keep cool and still have fun on a hot day.

ANOTHER PARTY IDEA

Lay blankets or sheets on grass for picnic.

SNO-CONES 🍧

Crush lots of cubes (made of orange juice or lemonade) in blender or ice crusher.
    or
Crush ice cubes (with 1/2 cup water) in blender.
Put in cups.
Add syrup:
  2 T. fruit juice concentrate

Sandwiches

✋ If there is a pool, a grown-up should watch small children.

ANOTHER PARTY IDEA

MENU

Orange Juice
Hot chocolate
Melon Slice with Ice Cream
Pancakes
Sausage

EARLY
BIRD PARTY
COME FOR
BREAKFAST
8:30 - 10:30
MARCH 10
CELIA'S HOUSE
1384 VALENCIA RD

Surprise Guest
(exercise instructor)
Arrives soon after guests
to lead warmup exercises
and jogging.

ALIBI

Object

To identify the robber
by listening to crazy alibis

Cards (use regular deck)
Ace — robber, K — victim,
Q — police person (plus as
many others as players)

Pass out cards. Victim reports
he/she has been robbed. Police
Officer begins questioning.
Suspects and robber give alibis.
After questioning, officer tries
to identify the robber. If he
fails after 3 tries, robber
surrenders and passes out cards
for next round.

BREAKFAST PARTY

Plan a morning party
with breakfast, games, and
some exercise. This is a
zippy way to wake up.

Comic book
favor

Decorate with
"early birds"

PANCAKE TIP..

The pancakes can
be stored in a warm
oven and served all
at once. Cover with a
clean dish towel to
prevent drying.

PAUL'S PANCAKES

1-1/2 cups of all purpose flour
1 t. salt
3 T. sugar
1-3/4 t. baking powder
2 eggs
   (Secret — separate whites and yolk,
   put yokes with milk. Beat whites
   until stiff, blend in whites last.)
3 T. melted butter, oil, or grease
1 to 1-1/4 cups milk

Pour onto preheated griddle (or frying
pan). If pancakes stick, grease griddle.

SPOT TAG

When you are tagged
you must hold the spot
where you were touched
until you catch someone.

101

SURPRISE

LUKE'S LUNCHEON PIZZAS
(serves 6)

6 English muffins
Spaghetti or pizza
   sauce, cheese, sliced
Toast muffins
Put sauce on top side
Lay cheese slice on top
Put under broiler till
   cheese melts.

PASSWORD 👁

(a good game for 4 to 10 players)

The object of this game is to successfully pass a word to your partner, using a one-word clue.

Everyone has a partner (if there's an uneven number, take turns keeping score). One of each partnership is an "A" and the other a "B."

An "A" writes down a word and shows it to all the "A" players (if someone cannot see or read, whisper the word to him/her).

The "A's" must take turns giving 1-word clues to their partners, until the word is guessed. Whoever thought up the word gives the clue last.

If the word is guessed the first time, the partnership wins 10 points, then 9, 8, and so on. Next time the "B's" think of a word. Someone must keep score.

No words with capital letters!

Can you find any old school or play pictures of your friend? How about a few home movies? (only show them if your friend thinks it's OK.)

SURPRISE BOOK

An imaginative gift to a sick friend — or one who's not sick. Buy a photo album with removable pages. A few days before the party, give an empty page to each guest. Each guest will fill the page with notes, photos, cutouts, or whatever he/she thinks the friend would enjoy.

The receiver of this book will treasure it! (This idea is also a perfect gift for someone who's moving away.)

Maybe the whole class could prepare a book for a friend or the teacher.

ANOTHER PARTY IDEA

SDRAWKCAB PARTY

It is great fun to do things backwards!

TO JOANNIE

PLEASE COME TO
MY PARTY

LYNN ST. IN
MONROE
ON APRIL 29

CHUCK

On back write:
Things at my party will
be upside down or backwards.
Please dress that way and
be prepared!

Say things in the wrong
order ("good bye"
when you mean "hello.")

UNEM
ICE CREAM CONE
(UPSIDE DOWN)
APPLE JUICE
SAM'S HAM BBQ
SANDWICHES

CHALK BOARD

SPECIAL ACTIVITIES

Arrange order of
party backwards.

Say things in the wrong
order ("good bye"
when you mean "hello."

Have guests come in back
door or window.

Food could be eaten under
the table.

Decorations could be
under the furniture.

GAMES

Relays — done backwards.
Write poem backwards.
Winners are losers.
Losers are winners.

SAM'S HAM BBQ SANDWICHES

To 1 lb. thinly sliced ham, add:
1/2 cup ketchup
1/4 cup vinegar
2 T. brown sugar
1/8 cup water
1/2 t. paprika
1/2 t. mustard
Heat and serve on rolls
(Serves 6)

DECORATIONS

Hang balloons under
the table.
Where possible change
furniture, pictures,
etc. to be backwards.

TAKE ALONG PARTY

Have a party for the friend (child or adult)
who is in bed or unable to get up and around.
It's fun to cheer up a friend.

R̶x DATE SEPT. 16.

PRESCRIPTION FOR: BILL
ADDRESS 12215 MOSSYCUP DR.

DOSAGE: 11:00 AM - 12:00.
DR. CASEY
OFFICE 491-6285

Take along a picnic basket
with sandwiches, juice,
carrots, celery, fruit,
brownies, paper plates,
cups, and napkins.

GIFT IDEAS

Comics
Crafts
Games
Pencil and paper
Game books
Books
Puppets
Clipboard

GAMES 🎲

Word games
  Buzz
  Grandmother's Trunk
Memory
Crazy Picture

Remember to: ✋
Check with an adult first
to see if it's OK.
Clean up when you leave.
Don't stay too long.

ANOTHER PARTY IDEA

OCTOPUS FAVOR

You could leave this with your friend (for company in bed!)

Need for 1 octopus:
Yarn (amount varies with size of octopus - 36 pieces of 36" yarn equals 1 octopus)
2-4 buttons
Cotton or batting (to stuff the head)

Instructions:
Cut 36 pieces of yarn 36 inches long (this can be done before the party.) Tie together in middle.
Arrange yarn around cotton head and tie at neck. Sew buttons for eyes and nose.
Braid remaining yarn into 8 legs. Use 9 strands or more for each leg.

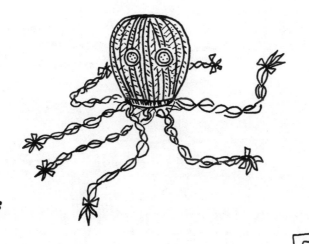

BUZZ – A NUMBER GAME

Each person states a number in succession beginning with one. Whenever the number 7 is used, or a multiple of 7 (like 14, 21, etc.), the person must say "Buzz" instead.

1-2-3-4-5-6-Buzz-8-9-10-11-12-13-Buzz-15-16-Buzz-18-19-20-Buzz-22-23 and so on.

BRIAN'S BROWNIES

2 squares unsweetened chocolate
1 stick margarine or shortening
2 eggs
1 cup sugar
1 t. vanilla
1/2 cup flour
1/8 t. salt

Melt chocolate with butter in saucepan.
Beat eggs till foamy in large bowl.
Add sugar gradually until thick (about 5 minutes.)
Stir in vanilla, chocolate, fold in flour and salt.
Spread in greased pan 8x8x2.
Bake 350° for 30 minutes.

1 · 2 · 3 · 4 · 5 · 6 · BUZZ

DOLL OR STUFFED ANIMAL PARTY

There could be a doll play area.
Set up a card table or a box as a stage.
If you have any doll carriages, cribs,
high chairs, or small chairs set them out.

Inside:
  Instead of buying a gift,
  bring a new outfit for
  your doll or animal (you
  could buy baby clothes at
  a thrift store or make an
  apron or a skirt).

TO KRISTINE

COME AND BRING
YOUR DOLL OR STUFFED
ANIMAL TO
RYAN AND MOLLY'S SAT. MAY 20
135 BEECHWOOD DRIVE

12 - 2:00

CENTER STAGE

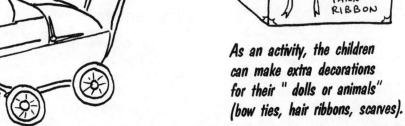

FABRICS
YARN
RIBBON

As an activity, the children
can make extra decorations
for their " dolls or animals"
(bow ties, hair ribbons, scarves).

TELEPHONE 🔘

Sit in a circle.
One person whispers a secret
   to the next.
Each person passes the
   secret along.
The last person says it
   aloud.
How the secret has changed!

COPY CAT 🔘

This is a game played
while sitting in a circle.
A secret "leader" is leading
movements made with the hands
and body while a guesser tries
to guess who is leading the
group's movements.

Instructions:

The guesser covers his/her eyes
or leaves the room while a leader
is chosen (perhaps by the birthday
person.) This leader starts a body
action (examples: clapping, patting
floor, clicking fingers, tapping floor
with feet, etc.) The other players
copy this action. The guesser returns
to the circle and tries to guess who
is leading the group. The leader
continually changes the movement.
The group tries to fool the guesser
by not looking directly at the
leader.

The guesser gets 3 guesses, then
he/she becomes the person to choose
the next leader and the former leader
becomes the guesser.

Put your dolls or
animals in the
circle, too.

107

DRESS-UP PARTY

Invite guests to dress up any way they wish. (This is a good way to try a new identity!)

ON THE BACK →

DRESS UP PARTY AT ARNOLD'S OCT 28 7:00 – 9:00 5 PHELPS DR.

DRESS UP IN A FUN OR CRAZY WAY! BE DARING!

GREG'S GINGERBREAD (CIDER, TOO!)

Beat:
    2 eggs
Add:
    1/2 cup molasses
    1/2 cup sour cream
    1/2 cup brown sugar
Beat well.
Sift together:

    1-1/2 cups flour
    1 t. baking soda
    1 t. ginger
    1/4 t. salt

Stir into first mixture.
Add 1/2 cup melted butter.
Beat well. Pour into 9"
    buttered pan.
Bake at 350º for 30 minutes.
(serves 9)

LORI'S LEMON SAUCE
(makes 1 cup)

Boil together for 5 minutes without stirring:
    3/4 cup sugar
    2 T. light corn syrup
    1/4 cup water

Remove pan from heat and add:
    2 T. lemon juice
    2 t. butter

Serve over gingerbread.

ANOTHER PARTY IDEA

GAMES

SHADOW

Hang old sheet in doorway
with light behind it.
Guests make movements
behind it.
Others guess who it is.

BABY FINGERS

Use an old sheet. Cut holes
for fingers.
The guests stick baby fingers
through the holes.
One person guesses who owns
the finger.

Dunk for apples

Favors — make puppets

Make out
of fabric
or paper

Award a prize
for each costume.

108

ANOTHER PARTY IDEA

CARNIVAL

This is a clever way to run your own carnival and to be a customer, too. Design your own games!

Kids can take turns running the booths or being the patrons. One child could run the restaurant, another could make the tickets.

RELAY RACES
Sack
Potato or tennis ball on a spoon
Jumping
Skipping
Running backwards

For booths use card tables or cardboard boxes

Toss in pennies, bottle caps, or other small objects.

A soda carton or case would do

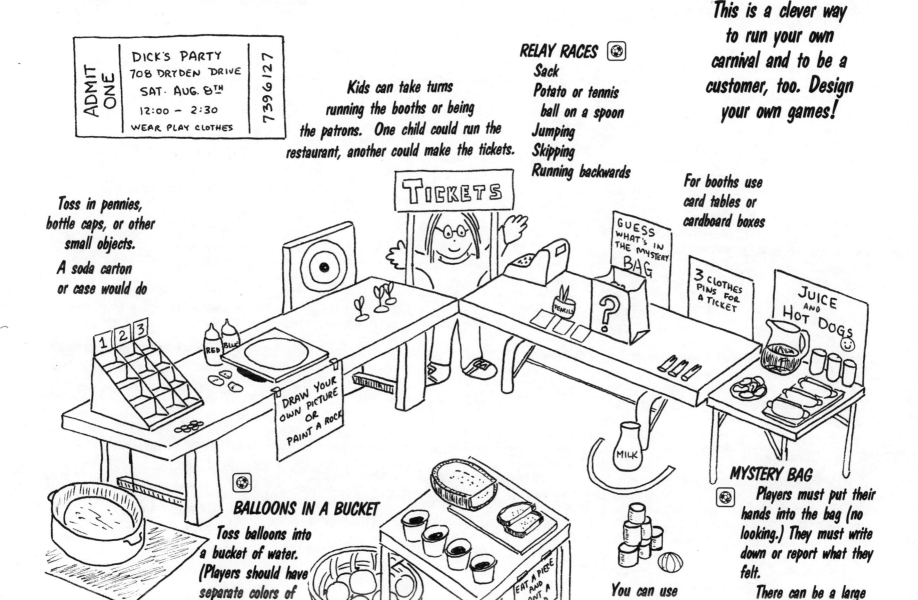

TICKETS

GUESS WHAT'S IN THE MYSTERY BAG

3 CLOTHES PINS FOR A TICKET

JUICE AND HOT DOGS

PENCILS

?

RED BLUE

DRAW YOUR OWN PICTURE OR PAINT A ROCK

MILK

1 2 3

EAT A PIECE AND PLANT A SEED

BALLOONS IN A BUCKET
Toss balloons into a bucket of water. (Players should have separate colors of balloons or have marked ones.)

You can use empty tins cans (remove lids) and rubber balls.

MYSTERY BAG
Players must put their hands into the bag (no looking.) They must write down or report what they felt.

There can be a large variety of items in the bag.

ANOTHER PARTY IDEA

MENU
SANDWICHES
COLD JUICE
ICE WATER
WATER MELON
ORANGE SLICES

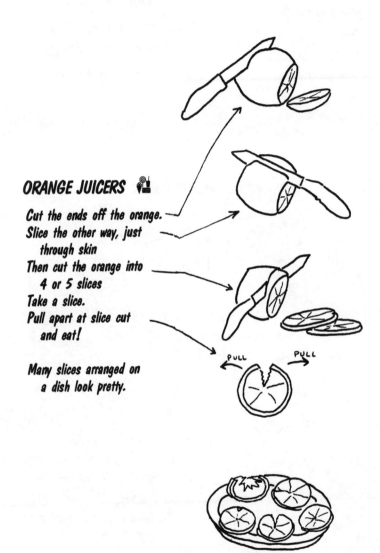

ORANGE JUICERS

Cut the ends off the orange.
Slice the other way, just
    through skin
Then cut the orange into
    4 or 5 slices
Take a slice.
Pull apart at slice cut
    and eat!

Many slices arranged on
    a dish look pretty.

PULL   PULL

MAY I, MOTHER?

Players try to get from a
starting line to a finish
line with permission from
leader (mother).
    Instructions:
        Leader instructs individual
        players to take a certain
        number of steps,* for example:
        "(Vinnie) please take 2 umbrella
        steps." Player must reply, "May
        I, Mother?" "Yes, you may."

*Steps (make up your own)
    Baby step
    Giant step
    Banana step (slide feet in
        shape of banana)
    Umbrella step (with hand on
        head, spin once)
    Bunny step (hop)

ONE GIANT STEP!

WATER BALLOON TOSS

Partners stand opposite one another. All the balloons are on one side. After the first throw (1 partner to the other,) the separating string is moved back a bit to separate the partners. The game continues until all the balloons are broken.

FIELD DAY
AT
SHERMAN SCHOOL
JULY 9   1- 3:00

RAIN DATE : THE NEXT NICE DAY

FROM MARA TO CHRIS

FINISH

Sack race

Water balloon toss

FIELD DAY

Plan an afternoon of races and outdoor fun.

Kids can take turns deciding what the races will be.

Three legged race

Rope (or use strips of fabric, like sheets, tied at ankle and above knee.)

Have balloons filled, rope or fabric scraps cut, and sacks ready in advance.

Favors — whistle on a string for around the neck.

Ring toss

Prizes should be small torches to pin on.

ANOTHER PARTY IDEA

THE PRICE IS CORRECT ⊚

This game is played with 2 teams. A player from one team guesses the price of selected items against one player from the other team.

Needed:

5 or so food items (examples: can of fruit, box of cereal, package of cookies, etc.)

Instructions:

One player from each team tries to guess the correct price of each item. The player coming closest to the correct total without going over the price wins points (you decide how many) for his/her team.

SLOPPY JOSIES

To 1 lb. ground beef, browned and drained add:

    1/2 cup ketchup
    1/3 cup water
    1 t. mustard
    1 t. worcestershire sauce
    1 t. salt
    1/2 t. pepper
    1 T. brown sugar
(serves 6)

Simmer 15 minutes or more.

ORVILLE'S ORANGE FLIPS

6 oz. can orange juice, frozen
1/2 cup milk
1/2 cup water
1/4 cup sugar
1/2 t. vanilla
6 ice cubes
1 egg

Blend for 1 minute in blender or shake well.
(serves 4)

DO IT YOURSELF — SHOP AND EAT

GROUP 1
Buy Sloppy Josie
ingredients
Prepare
Clean up

SHOPPING
GROUP 2
LETTUCE ✓
SPINACH ✓
OIL
VINEGAR ✓
1 CUCUMBER
1 TOMATO

After the guests arrive, they are divided into groups. Each group is given a shopping list and an envelope of money. After shopping, everyone returns and prepares the food for dinner. All clean up and then eat!

GROUP 2
Buy salad ingredients
Prepare
Clean up

After each group buys
the food, they seal the
change in an envelope
and give it to the adult.

CHANGE

Remove lable from can.
Write invitation on back.

JUICE
ALL
NATURAL
100% #

ROGER'S HOUSE
703 UNION ST.
NOVEMBER 6TH
11:00 — 2:00
R.S.V.P. 363-1242

GROUP 3
Buy orange flip
ingredients
Prepare
Clean up

MENU

Sloppy Josies on Buns
Tossed Salad
Potato Chips
Orange Flips
Cupcakes

GROUP 4
Buy cupcake
ingredients
Prepare
Clean up

GROUP 5
Buy paper plates, cups,
napkins, and peanuts for
nut cups
Set table

Be well organized before friends come.
Prepare shopping lists, recipes, and envelopes
containing money for each group.
Prepare kitchen spots for each group with
all necessary items.

ANOTHER PARTY IDEA

FRANK'S FRIED CHICKEN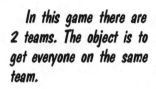

1-3 lb. chicken, cut in pieces
1-1/2 cups flour
3/4 t. baking powder
pepper and salt to taste

Dip each piece into milk
and then coat with the flour,
baking powder, and seasonings.

Fry chicken in 1-1/2" to 2"
cooking oil or shortening in
in frying pan, about 40 minutes
to an hour or until golden brown.

BETH'S BAKED CHICKEN
(Serves 6)

1-3 lb. chicken cut up in pieces
1 egg, beaten
1-1/2 cups flour
1 t. poultry seasoning
salt and pepper to taste
1/4 lb. butter or margarine, melted

Set over at 350°
Dip pieces of chicken into egg
and then into a bag with the flour,
poultry seasoning, pepper, and salt.
Place chicken in a 9" x 13" pan
and pour melted butter over the top.
Cover with aluminum foil and bake
for 30 min. Remove foil and bake
uncovered for 30 min. more.

GERT'S GERMAN POTATO SALAD

1 pound pork sausages (optional)
5 strips bacon
1/2 cup chopped onion
1/3 cup chopped celery
1 t. salt
1/2 t. sugar
1/8 t. pepper
1/4 t. dry mustard
1/2 cup water
1/3 cup vinegar
4 cups sliced cooked potatoes
2 T. mayonnaise

Fry bacon until crisp, saute
onions and celery in bacon
drippings. Drain grease.
Add salt, sugar, pepper, dry
mustard, water and vinegar.
Crumble bacon and add
potatoes and mayonnaise to
sauce.
Bake at 300° for 20 minutes.
Top with cooked sausage,
if desired.

In this game there are
2 teams. The object is to
get everyone on the same
team.

LEMONADE

Instructions:
Players stand in 2 lines
far away from each other.
(Use string to mark boundaries.)
The players advance towards
one another a few steps at a
time, saying these words:
   Team 1 "Here we come!"
   Team 2 "Where from?"
   Team 1 "Phoenix, Arizona."
     (make up any name
     ahead of time)
   Team 2 "What's your trade?"
   Team 1 "Lemonade"
   Team 2 "Show us some if you're
     not afraid!"
By now everyone is standing in the
middle of the marked off area.
Everyone on Team 1 now pretends to
be doing a trade. (This trade should
be agreed upon by the whole team
before they started to march forward!)
No one on Team 1 can talk — you must do
your trade without words (a trade could
be "cleaning coins," "chopping wood,"
anything!) As soon as someone on
Team 2 guesses the trade correctly,
Team 1 must run to their starting line.
If you are caught, you must join the
other team. Next time, Team 2 thinks
of a trade and city. Sides take turns
having a trade.

ALPHABET HIKE

Find items for alphabet letters (examples, a-acorn, b-buttercup, c-cat tail) place in small bags. If you don't want to collect items, write what you saw on paper.

FOLLOW THE LEADER

If path is narrow and/or busy, ride to the right.

ZOOM TO SCOTT'S
DINNER TO PARK PICNIC
BRING BIKE 4-6:00

BIKE PATH PARTY

This party combines bike riding and picnicking. You might come across some interesting sights as a bonus!

You could have the picnic before or after the ride.

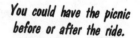

MENU FRIED CHICKEN POTATO SALAD FRESH FRUIT CUPCAKES ICE WATER

BIKE DECORATING

Have crepe paper for streamers, winding through wheels, etc.

✋ Cyclists should know ahead of time that following a slow moving bike, without crashing into it or making a fuss, is quite a remarkable skill! It's a more peaceful ride that way, too.

ANOTHER PARTY IDEA

OLLIE'S OVEN STEW

2 lb. stew beef
2 t. salt
1/4 t. pepper
1/4 t. paprika
2 T. oil
Onions
Carrots
Potatoes
Celery Sticks ⎬ 3-4 each, cut up
2-8 oz. cans tomato sauce
1 cup water

NOW ADD THE SEASONINGS.

Put beef into oven pot, mix with oil.
Bake for 30 minutes at 400°, uncovered.
Add vegetables, tomato sauce and water.
Cover. Bake for 2 hours at 350°.
(Serves 6 to 8)

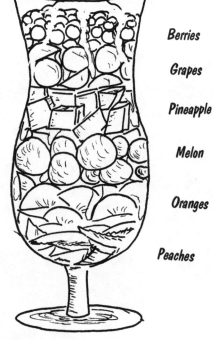

Berries

Grapes

Pineapple

Melon

Oranges

Peaches

FRUIT PARFAIT

Mix fruits layered.
(You could layer
    whipped cream too.)

INDOOR SCAVENGER HUNT

Hide about 10 items in a room.
The guests write down the list
of what's to be found. When they
find an item, it must not be
moved. Just check the list (✓).
The first one to find all the
items wins. Wait till everyone
is done.

FAVOR:
CLOVE BALL
(for sweet smelling closets and drawers)

Need:
    Boxes of whole cloves
    Orange for each guest
    Ribbon, or yarn — enough
        for hanging it
    Pins

Tie orange with ribbon, secured
with pins. Cover whole orange
with cloves. You can stick cloves
in ribbon to cover completely.

MENU

Limeade
Ollie's Oven Stew
French Bread
Fruit Parfait

GAMES 🌐

Indoor scavenger hunt
Word games
Who Am I?

WHO AM I? 🌐

Have famous names written
on cards. Tape or pin one
to each person's back.
Everyone walks around asking
questions (with yes or no
answers) of the others to
try to figure out who is
written on his/her back.

This is a good
game to play at the
beginning of the
party. It helps
people to get to
know one another.

*Invitation is written
on a napkin.*

DINNER PARTY
AT DANELLE'S
HOUSE
605 WEST STATE
DATE FEB. 11

TIME 6:00 - 8:00

DINNER PARTY

This party could be
fancy or plain, depending
on your menu, and where
you plan to eat. The kitchen
or the dining room (or wherever
else is best) would be fine.
You could set the table early,
or have your friends help.
Bon apetit!

SLEDDING PARTY

If you get some snow, this is a wonderful way to have a party!
Happy Sledding!

SOCK SLIPPERS

Need:

- 1 pair new long socks
- 2 pieces of felt (any color) cut to the foot size
- 4 sew-on eyes
    (eyes can also be made from buttons or felt)
- 1 ft. of ribbon
- Needle and thread

Instructions:

Cut felt to foot size. Sew on bottom of socks. Sew on eyes and bowed ribbon. Sew on felt in shape of mouth.

When the slipper becomes a puppet, the felt on bottom is the mouth (don't add a separate mouth).

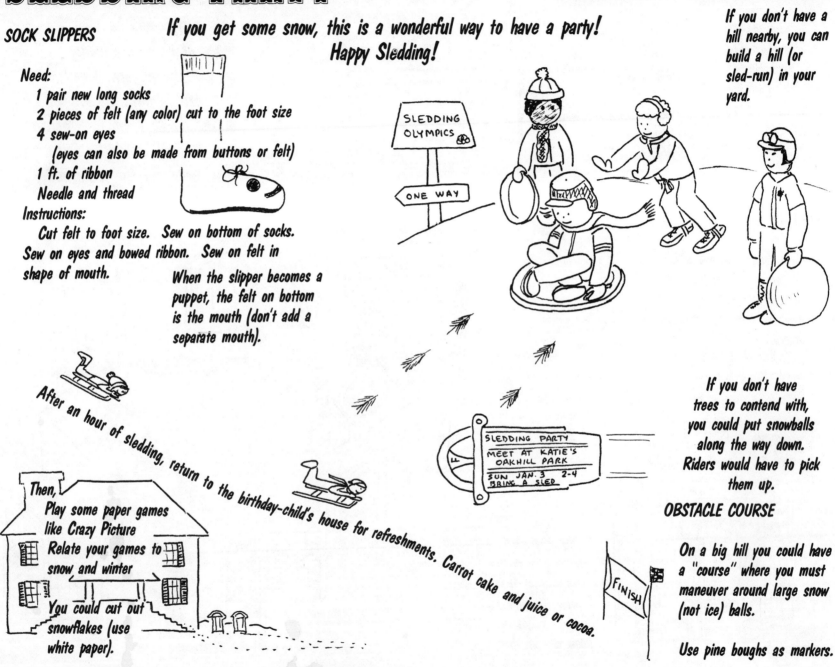

If you don't have a hill nearby, you can build a hill (or sled-run) in your yard.

After an hour of sledding, return to the birthday-child's house for refreshments. Carrot cake and juice or cocoa.

Then,

Play some paper games like Crazy Picture

Relate your games to snow and winter

You could cut out snowflakes (use white paper).

SLEDDING PARTY
MEET AT KATIE'S OAKHILL PARK
SUN JAN. 3 2-4
BRING A SLED

If you don't have trees to contend with, you could put snowballs along the way down. Riders would have to pick them up.

OBSTACLE COURSE

On a big hill you could have a "course" where you must maneuver around large snow (not ice) balls.

Use pine boughs as markers.

ANOTHER PARTY IDEA

A SPECIAL SHARING BIRTHDAY PARTY
AT DAN'S
1008 CLUE DRIVE
APT 4C
SAT. OCT 23 1-3:00

BRING SCISSORS AND A PACKAGE OF CANDY OR NUTS. WE WILL TAKE YOU HOME AFTER OUR VISIT TO THE NURSING HOME

Popcorn
for
snack
Cranberry
juice or
Cider

Another possible favor for another day

1 CLOSET SACHET

2 yds. twine
1 yd. yarn (thick or thin)
2-3 bars or balls of soap
2-3 fabric squares (calico is cute),
big enough to cover soap

Fold twine at middle.
Tie three knots, evenly
   spaced.
Cover soap with fabric,
   tie with yarn.
Tie wrapped soaps to
   knots (use extra yarn
   or slip fabric into
   loosened knot.)

You could make favors like puppets, notebooks, or peanut people to take when you visit your friend.

KINDNESS PARTY

This is a party where you can have fun, learn a craft, and cheer someone else up, too!

Set table with supplies.
Cover with newspapers
   or something old.

SNACK JAR

Any size jar (baby food
   jars are nice)
Felt around the edge
Acrylic paint for the words

Check with the hospital or nursing home (or with whomever you're sharing) and arrange your delivery time (like 3:00 Saturday afternoon).
Tell how many favors you'll be bringing.

ANOTHER PARTY IDEA

TIC TAC TOES ⊚

This is like the paper
game only played with
people. #

Need:

   9 plain squares of paper
      (to lay on floor)
   Papers marked X or O to
      divide equally among players
   List of questions, prepared
      before the party (include
      fun ones about school,
      teachers, town, etc.)

Instructions:

   Divide players into 2 teams (X's and O's)
   An adult asks questions
      "What is your teacher's first name?"
   If player answers correctly, he/she
      stands on paper in the position
      of choice. (Player holds an "X"
      or "O" paper.)
   If wrong, the same question is
      asked of the next team.
   The same question is only asked
      twice.
   Three X's or O's in a row first wins.

HILLARY'S HOT COCOA 🔥

Mix in saucepan
   1/4 c. cocoa
   2 T. sugar
   pinch salt
Add 1/2 cup boiling water
Boil 3 minutes
Add 4 cups milk
Heat slowly. When hot but not
   boiling, beat until frothy.
Add 1 t. vanilla.
(serves 6-8)

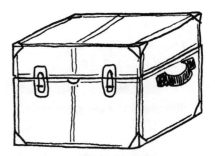

GRANDMA'S TRUNK ⊚

This is a memory game.
Take turns making up and trying
to remember what is in her trunk.
A - apple, B - boots, C - cap
through Z.
Each person must repeat
all previously mentioned items
before adding his alphabet
contribution to the trunk.

COOKIE EXCHANGE

Each guest brings 3 dozen cookies
   in a container.
All cookies are placed on a table
   on plates (paper would do.)
Each guest uses his/her empty
   container to choose 2-1/2
   dozen to take home.
The rest are served at party!

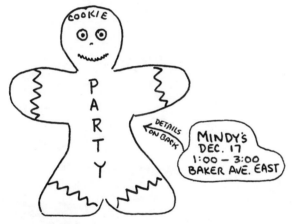

COOKIE

P
A
R
T
Y

DETAILS
ON BACK

MINDY'S
DEC. 17
1:00 — 3:00
BAKER AVE. EAST

DECORATIONS

Pretty table set for exchange.
Gingerbread persons cut out of
   brown paper on door and table.

FAVORS

Spoon dolls
Each guest gets a wooden spoon.
Supply a box of scrap fabric,
   yarn, ribbon, markers.

COOKIE EXCHANGE

Each guest brings 1 kind of cookie
and then has a variety to take home!
This is a cozy
indoor party.

HOT
COCOA

REFRESHMENTS

Hot cocoa

Popcorn (not buttered)

Hamburgers (foil would keep
them hot)

(Possibly beans, to be like
winter campers.) NOVELTY: kids
could eat them out of discarded
cleaned tin cans — lids removed.
Use spoon or fork. Hold cans
with mittens.

If it's not too freezing cold, an outdoor winter party with lots of different activities would be a lot of fun and refreshing!

FORT HENRY

Snow packed
on tree
for
target

If snow is fresh, roll
big balls for
climbing

The kids can build
a snow home.
(Don't put a roof on,
for safety's sake.)

ANOTHER PARTY IDEA

Have some shaping tools

SEARCH PARTY

Each of 2 teams can hide a "treasure" in the snow. The others must go on an expedition to find it. (An empty can — label removed, can be lost silver.)

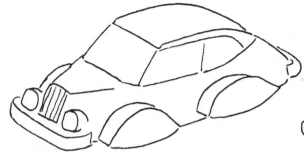

Shovels

Garden tools

Pail

SNOW SCULPTURE

Work alone or with others. Everyone could work on 1 sculpture, like a car.

FIND THE "ICE CUBE"

Ice cubes could be hidden all around the yard. Later on kids could take turns hiding and finding 1 particular cube. (You might want to color them beforehand.)

Kids can give each other rides on a sled. They can deliver each other to different areas.

RELAY GAMES OUTSIDE

- **SNOW SHOVEL RELAY**
  Two teams on driveway (snowy ones) shovel up and back. The clearest half of driveway wins.

- **PULL PERSON ON SLED UP AND BACK**

- **BAG OF HATS, SCARFS AND MITTENS**
  Run up, put on, run back, take off. (See Suitcase Relay)

SKATING PARTY

If you have a free skating area nearby, that's fortunate! If not, you might have to pay admission fees at an indoor rink. (If your friends don't have skates, you could help them find some to borrow.) Happy Skating!

TIP MAKE THIS BATTER BEFORE THE PARTY. WHEN YOU RETURN FROM SKATING, POUR AND BAKE THE MUFFINS

BRING SKATES AT CENTRAL PARK POND
FEB 17 1-3
SKATING PARTY AT DOMINIC'S 11 EAST ST

Take along someone who can skate well and who could give a few skating tips.

GRANNIE FRANNIE'S BRANNIES
(makes about 36 muffins)

2 eggs
1/2 cup vegetable oil
1-1/2 cups sugar
2-1/2 cups flour
2-1/2 t. baking soda
2 t. salt
1 t. cinnamon
2 cups buttermilk
4-1/2 cups raisin bran

Hot Cider

Spiced Cider

Cocoa

A pond or lake with ice approximately 8" thick. It should be frozen for 3 weeks. (You could create your own skating rink in a yard, too.)

Do Figure Eights

Mix together eggs, oil, and sugar.
Add flour, baking soda, salt and cinnamon.
Stir in buttermilk, then raisin bran.
Bake at 400° for 20 minutes.
(This batter lasts for 6 weeks in the refrigerator. Keep in a sealed container and bake as you need them.)

DECORATIONS
Homemade snowflakes on table
(White on colored sheet or vice versa)

Skating to music is fun (portable radios might work in a small area).

Learning to skate backwards and to turn around are great feats to accomplish!

Play Follow-the-Leader on ice! Take turns being leader.

Older kids might like to play hockey.

124

PARTY TIPS

TIPS FOR PARTY GUESTS

Try to eat what's served. Don't be a picky eater.

If you don't want to play a game, offer to help or watch quietly.

Be a good sport.

TIPS FOR THE BIRTHDAY PERSON

Sometimes all of the kids you invited can't come. Enjoy the ones who do come!

To avoid hurt feelings, don't deliver your invitations in school unless you're inviting the whole class. It is better to write and mail, phone, or hand deliver them.

Try to say Hi and Goodbye to each guest.

If a guest is not being his/her nicest self, don't let that ruin your party. (He/she might need a special job at that point! Enjoy the rest of the guests and activities!)

OFTEN THE 1 OR 2 KIDS YOU WEREN'T GOING TO INVITE, ARE THE HAPPIEST TO BE INVITED

TIPS FOR PARENTS

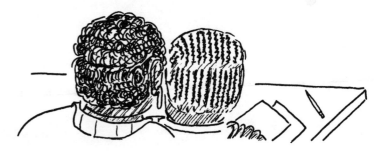

Make party plans with your child. Then you will both know what to expect.

The better prepared you are ahead of time, the easier things will be later (like, if you will be needing scissors for the kids, have them ready beforehand in a certain spot.)

Have a list of party activities and their approximate times.

If you are having a large group, you will probably need help from a neighbor, relative or older child (the more compatible, the better.)

Have extra games in mind in case your 2 hour party is over in 45 minutes. Many popular games require no special supplies, like Old Witch, Cat and Mouse, Telephone, card games, etc. The children might suggest some favorites.

Be realistic:
    Have foods that kids like.
    Don't plan too little or too much.
    Be willing to change an activity if it's going poorly.

If you look like you're relaxed and enjoying the party, the children will feel more comfortable.

If a child is difficult, handle the situation at the moment (it's too short a time to try to reform the child; however, don't hesitate to be firm — to a point.)

Children are often better behaved if they can participate in preparing the food or doing a craft. They needn't be served.

Often the birthday-child can act out-of-sorts. Try to be extra nice to him/her during the party. No one will mind and everything will go more smoothly.

CLEANUP

The guests might enjoy carrying their dishes and scraps to the kitchen.

If someone offers to help during the party, perhaps he/she could clean up after each activity. It's quite a treat to find everything all in order again.

Have a bag or box for trash. You can save the ribbons and paper which didn't rip. You can re-use them. (Set aside a special drawer, box or bag for wrappings - it's a big help and saves time and money.)

Check after the party for what's out of order. Cleaning up right away is usually a good idea.

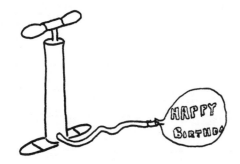

Don't run or play games and eat at the same time. It's best to sit and eat quietly.

Small children should not blow up balloons. Older children and adults are best suited for that. Throw balloon scraps in trash.

Don't serve hard candy or nuts to small children at a party.

When the party's over, watch that each child gets safely on his/her way. (Mostly watch that no one runs into the street.)

ON NOT BEING INVITED

If you don't get invited to someone's party, try to remember that:

No one gets invited to everyone's party.
It doesn't mean that the child doesn't like you.
Sometimes the child can only have a few friends.
Sometimes the parents have decided who can come.
There could be other reasons.
   (Your host might even have forgotten!)
It happens to everyone. For sure!

YOU'D GO BROKE IF YOU WENT TO EVERY PARTY !

YOM MOLEDET SOMAYACH

BUON COMPLEANNO

HARTELIJK GEFELICITEERD

FELIZ CUMPLEAÑOS

JOYEAUX ANNIVERSAIRE

GRATULERER MED DAGEN

GLÜCKLICHER GEBURTSTAG

TIL LYKKE

誕
生
日

誕
生
日
お
め
で
と
う

JAPANESE

مبارک گل جنم

URDU PAKISTANI

जन्म दिन
मुबारक

HINDUSTANI

mừng ngày

sinh nhật

VIETNAMESE

GELUK MET JOU

VERJAARS DAG.

AFRIKAANS

WESOLYCH URODZIEN   **POLISH**

당신의 생일을 축하합니다

KOREAN

HAPPY BIRTHDAY!

ENGLISH

INDEX

If you are looking for a game or recipe mentioned in this book, you can look up the title and page number in the Index.

(By the way, in the 4 parties photographed for this book, there are more activities shown than you could accomplish in 2 hours. Just select some of the ideas for your party.)

THEMES

found in this book

GAMES

found in this book

(The age categories are not hard and fast; many of the games can be played by all ages.)

FOOD

found in this book

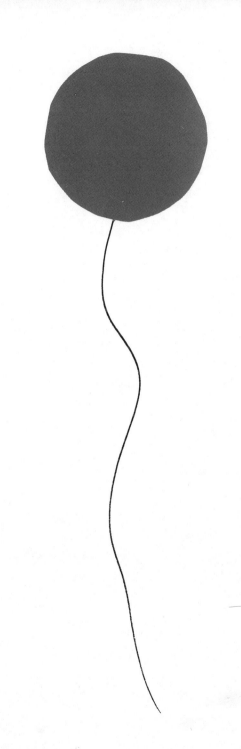

THE END

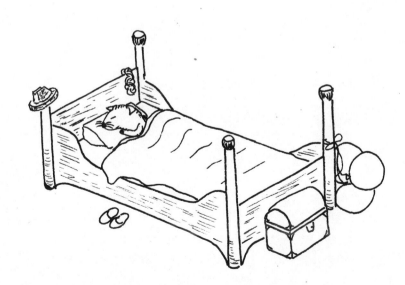